W9-DEF-277

SYSTEMS OF GOVERNMENT
DEMOCRACY

Alex Woolf

WORLD ALMANAC® LIBRARY

Please visit our web site at: www.worldalmanaclibrary.com
For a free color catalog describing World Almanac® Library's list of high-quality books
and multimedia programs, call 1-800-848-2928 (USA) or 1-800-387-3178 (Canada).
World Almanac® Library's fax: (414) 332-3567.

Library of Congress Cataloging-in-Publication Data

Woolf, Alex, 1964-
    Democracy / by Alex Woolf.
        p. cm. — (Systems of government)
    Includes bibliographical references and index.
    ISBN 0-8368-5883-2 (lib. bdg.)
    ISBN 0-8368-5888-3 (softcover)
    1. Democracy—Juvenile literature. 2. Democracy—History—Juvenile literature.
    I. Title. II. Series.
    JC423.W63   2005
    321.8—dc22

2005042116

This North American edition first published in 2006 by
World Almanac® Library
A Member of the WRC Media Family of Companies
330 West Olive Street, Suite 100
Milwaukee, WI 53212 USA

This edition copyright © 2006 by World Almanac® Library. First published by Evans Brothers Limited.
Copyright © 2005 by Evans Brothers Limited, 2A Portman Mansions, Chiltern Street, London W1U 6NR,
United Kingdom. This U.S. edition published under license from Evans Brothers Limited.

Editor: Patience Coster
Designer: Jane Hawkins
Illustrations: Stefan Chabluk
Consultant: Michael Rawcliffe

World Almanac® Library editorial direction: Mark J. Sachner
World Almanac® Library art direction: Tammy West
World Almanac® Library production: Jessica Morris
World Almanac® Library editor: Gini Holland
World Almanac® Library designer: Kami Koenig

Photo credits: We are grateful to the following for permission to reproduce photographs: Archivo
Iconografico, S.A./Corbis 12; Baldwin H. Ward and Kathryn C. Ward/Corbis 11; Horacio Villalobos/Corbis 28;
Leonard de Selva/Corbis 17; Rex front cover and 33; Rex/Boris Bocheinski 5; Rex/CA 29; Rex/CNP 25, 36;
Rex/EVT 21; Rex/MBF 9; Rex/NYP 40; Rex/SIPA 4, 23 (both), title page and 30, 41, 42-3; Topham/Feltz 20;
Topham/Fotomas 14; Topham/ImageWorks front cover and 6, 27, 35, 38; Topham Picturepoint 10, 15, 19, 26,
32; Topham/Polfoto 18; Topham/Press Association 39; Topham/UPPA 34.

Printed in the United States of America

1 2 3 4 5 6 7 8 9 09 08 07 06 05

CONTENTS

This book uses the general term *state* when referring to all the varieties of independent political units (country, nation, federation, empire) and is not to be confused with the smaller units within some countries that are also called states, such as the fifty states making up the United States. Dates in this book are written using B.C.E. and C.E. instead of B.C. and A.D. The letters B.C.E. stand for "Before the Common Era" and replace B.C. ("Before Christ"). The letters C.E. stand for "in the Common Era" and they replace A.D. ("Anno Domini," which is Latin for "in the year of our Lord").

CHAPTER ONE

WHAT IS DEMOCRACY?

During the course of our lives, we make many decisions on our own as individuals, such as what to eat, when to go to sleep, or what to watch on TV. We must also make decisions as members of a group, be it our family, our school, our neighborhood, or our country. In these situations, we must find appropriate ways of making decisions. For example, we can allow one person in the group to decide everything, or we can try to agree on things together. Democracy is a system in which people decide matters together, or collectively, by voting. It is a system that can be applied to any of the groups mentioned above. As a system of government, democracy, more than any other governmental system, gives citizens a voice and considerable power to direct political matters locally, nationally, and internationally.

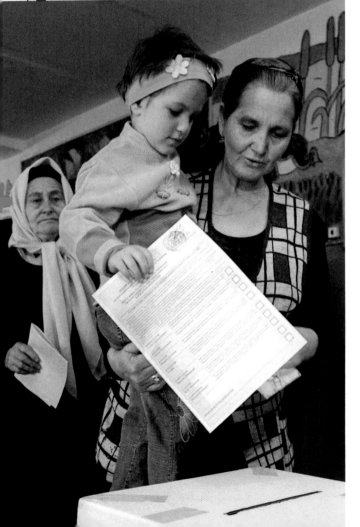

The word "democracy" was invented by the ancient Greeks, who were the first people known to take this idea of collective decision-making and turn it into a system of government. They combined their words *demos* (people) and *krates* (rule) to form *democracy*, or "rule by the people." So, in a democracy, the people rule. They are sovereign, meaning that they are the highest authority in the land. This approach contrasts with other forms of government, such as authoritarianism and communism, where sovereignty and power rest with an individual or a small group. People living in a democracy are generally more politically free than those living under other systems of government because they can exercise more control over the way they are governed.

◄ People in the Russian Republic of Chechnya vote in 2003. This simple act of writing a cross next to a favored candidate on a voting paper and placing the paper in a box is practiced in much the same way in countries all over the world.

◀ The right to protest (part of the right to freedom of speech) is fundamental to all democracies, even if the message is one with which most people strongly disagree—as in the case of this demonstration by German right-wing extremists.

REPRESENTATIVE DEMOCRACY

In an ideal democracy, each person plays his or her part in every decision about the laws and policies of the country. People attend regular meetings where the issues are debated, and then they vote according to their opinions. This approach is democracy in its purest form, and it is known as "direct democracy."

Direct democracy can work well in small groups, such as clubs and societies, or even in very small countries with few inhabitants. Direct democracy is not practical, however, in today's world, with state populations often numbering in the millions and with people too busy to be concerned with the details of every political issue.

Modern democratic countries have therefore adopted a system known as "representative democracy." Under this system, the people elect representatives to make decisions on their behalf. Every few years, an election is held, and the people get the chance to vote for representatives. The candidates (people wishing to become representatives) at these elections are usually members of a political party—an organization of people with similar, but not neces-

> "Any law which the people has not ratified [approved] in person is void; it is not law at all. The English people believes itself to be free; it is gravely mistaken; it is free only during the election of Members of Parliament; as soon as the Members are elected, the people is enslaved; it is nothing."

The words of eighteenth-century political philosopher, Jean-Jacques Rousseau, in his book, *The Social Contract* (1762), Rousseau believed that only direct democracy could provide true political freedom.

sarily identical, views about how the country should be run. If, once elected, the representatives do not act according to the people's wishes, they may be voted out of office at the next election.

BRANCHES OF GOVERNMENT

So how does democracy work in practice? There are three different branches of government in a representative democracy. The executive (confusingly also known as "the government" in some

5

▲ U.S. president George W. Bush delivers a speech on the national budget to a joint session of Congress on February 27, 2001. The meeting includes members of the U.S. Senate and the House of Representatives.

countries, such as the UK) initiates and carries out policy. This first branch of government is led by the chief executive, who is known by various titles (for example, president, prime minister, or chancellor) in different countries. He or she heads a cabinet, or group of ministers, each of whom is responsible for a specific area of policy.

The second branch of government is the legislature, which debates and approves laws arising from the policies of the executive. It usually consists of two assemblies (gatherings) of elected representatives. Legislative assemblies have names such as Congress (United States), Parliament (**United Kingdom [UK]**), and National Assembly (France). The third branch is the judiciary (the courts), which is responsible for deciding legal arguments. The judiciary also judges disputes about interpretations of the law.

In many democracies, there is another function of government, known as "head of state." Usually given the title of monarch, the person who holds this ceremonial office has no real political power. The head of state's main role is to represent the country on state occasions and act as a force for unity in times of national crisis or division.

In a healthy democracy, the three branches of government should remain independent of one another, checking and balancing each other so that too much power does not rest in one place. An independent legislature will be more effec-

CONSTITUTIONS

A constitution is a set of rules and principles that lays down how a nation should be governed. Constitutions determine when elections should be held, the powers of the various offices of state, and how laws should be made. Constitutions place limits on the powers of government and guarantee the political rights and freedoms of individuals. They are a crucial element in any democracy, because, without them, governments might behave in an authoritarian way. Most constitutions, such as that of the United States, are written down in a single document. Some constitutions, such as the United Kingdom's, are described as "unwritten." In these cases, political behavior is governed by historical customs, laws, and habits.

tive at looking at the policies and actions of the executive. Similarly, a judiciary that is free of interference from the executive is less likely to make politically motivated judgements.

DIFFERENT SYSTEMS

There are several different types of representative democracy. In a presidential system (as in the United States, France, and most Latin American countries), the government (known as the president) and the legislative assembly are kept apart. The president does not sit in the legislative assembly, and there are separate elections for

"Democracy substitutes election by the incompetent many for appointment by the corrupt few."

A view from the author and playwright George Bernard Shaw suggesting that there were severe disadvantages to both democracy and authoritarianism and little to recommend either system.

government and legislature. Under this system, the president combines the roles of chief executive with head of state.

In a parliamentary system (as in the UK, Ireland, Germany, and India), the government and legislature are not kept separate. There is one election for both of them. The government sits in the legislative assembly (known as parliament) and is determined by which political party gets the most seats in parliament. Under this system, there is a separate head of state. He or she may either be directly elected, appointed by parliament, or be determined by heredity (as in constitutional monarchies like the UK, Belgium, and Spain).

▼ The different branches of government in a democracy all have lines of responsibility that flow between them, the electorate, and the constitution.

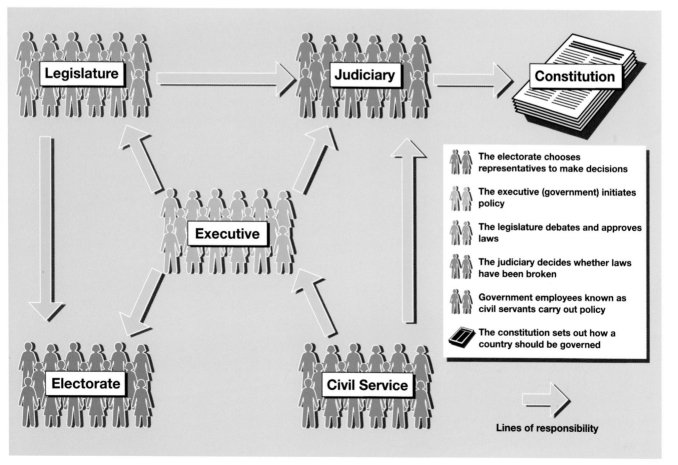

- The electorate chooses representatives to make decisions
- The executive (government) initiates policy
- The legislature debates and approves laws
- The judiciary decides whether laws have been broken
- Government employees known as civil servants carry out policy
- The constitution sets out how a country should be governed

Lines of responsibility

POLITICAL RIGHTS AND RESPONSIBILITIES

Democracy is not just about voting once every four or five years. If this were the case, then people would not be able to influence the affairs of their nationor protest against the actions of the government during the long periods in between elections.

Another important element of democracy is political rights. These include the right to say and write what one likes, to go where one pleases, to live in privacy and security, and to not be arrested or imprisoned without due legal process. All these sound like reasonable rights and freedoms to expect, and, in the vast majority of cases, they are.

FREEDOM OF THE PRESS

A safeguard of any democracy is a free press. Newspapers, radio, television, and the Internet, collectively known as the media, can be a very effective counterbalancing force, or check, on the power of the government. The government faces other checks on its power, of course, such as the legislature and the constitution. In the modern world, however, the media provides a crucial link between the government and the people.

In a well-functioning democracy, the media should be free to inform citizens of government actions, criticize the government, and provoke public debate on the key issues of the day. With this right, however, comes an obligation: The media must behave responsibly in its reporting the news and respect the rights of innocent individuals not to have their privacy invaded or their reputations damaged.

The problem arises when these rights conflict with the interests of the nation as a whole or with the rights or interests of another person or group. For example, does the right of free speech allow someone to incite (encourage) people to act violently against ethnic minorities? Most people would say it does not, because, in this case, the right to speak freely conflicts with the more fundamental right to live in safety without fear of being attacked. What this example shows is that rights are not all of equal value: Some rights can override others.

To give another example, does a convicted burglar have the right to freedom of movement? Certainly not, because this right conflicts with the duty of the government to protect its citizens from having their property stolen. In this case, the right of an individual has clashed with the interests of society. One of the ongoing debates in any democracy is how to balance the rights o f the individual with the rights of others, or with the national or social interest. Sometimes this balance is not straightforward. For example, should a person suspected of terrorism be locked up without a trial just in case he or she might carry out an attack?

These examples also illustrate the fact that in a democratic society, rights come with responsibilities. People cannot expect their rights to be respected when they do not act in a responsible way toward other people and towards society as a whole.

POLITICAL EQUALITY AND THE RULE OF LAW

There are two other key principles which, if ignored, would make democratic government impossible. The first is political equality. In other words, every mature person in the country, regardless of race, religious belief, or gender, has the same political rights as everyone else. The other key principle is the rule of law, which means that every person, whatever his or her status, must always act within the law and the constitution. The rule of law is a

The scene following a terrorist bomb attack on Madrid, Spain, in March 2004. Is it possible that the imprisonment of people who are suspected of being terrorists could prevent some of these tragedies from occurring in the future? Locking people up for long periods of time without trial goes against democratic principles, so democracies struggle to find other ways of dealing with this kind of threat.

guarantee to the people that those they have elected to represent them will not abuse the powers they have been given. For example, a chief executive may demand extra powers to tackle a national crisis. The chief executive, however, is not "above the law" and must first wait for the elected legislature to pass legislation (laws) to authorize the temporary use of such powers.

CHAPTER TWO

DEMOCRACY THROUGH THE AGES

A look back at history shows us that democracy is actually a fairly rare form of government. The vast majority of governments in past eras were authoritarian, dominated by a single leader—be it a monarch, a pharaoh, or an emperor—or a powerful élite (ruling group).

ANCIENT GREECE

Democracy appeared for the first time in the city-states of ancient Greece, most notably in Athens, between the sixth and fourth centuries B.C.E. A class of wealthy citizens emerged who employed slaves to work the land and do many of the other daily chores. Wealth and slaves gave the citizens time and energy to devote to other pursuits, including public affairs. They put pressure on the tyrants who ruled the city-states to give more power to the citizenry, and laws were reformed to allow this. In 620 B.C.E., tyrants introduced harsh laws, causing widespread resentment. The resented laws, combined with economic problems, threatened to destabilize the state. The tyrants were forced to make concessions to the citizenry, including giving them a say in running the government. In Athens, by the fifth century B.C.E., all citizens could attend an assembly, where they could vote on laws. Everyday matters were decided by a Council of Five Hundred. Citizens could also serve as jurors in the courts.

Athens boasted a higher level of popular participation than today's democracies and came close to Rousseau's ideal of a direct democracy (*see page 5*). Laws were made that prevented ambitious individuals or groups from becoming too powerful. For example, members of the Council were not elected but were chosen by lot. This random system prevented the Council from becoming dominated by ambitious individuals or groups. Also, most offices could not be held by the same person for more than two years in a row. Athenian democracy, however, fell short of modern democratic standards in one crucial respect: In Athens, only male citizens were allowed to vote and hold political office. The system excluded women and slaves.

PERICLES

Pericles (c.495–429 B.C.E.) was one of the greatest champions of Athenian democracy. He led a successful campaign to restrict the powers of the Areopagus, an unelected council of elders, rather like the Roman Senate. He also reformed the jury system, introducing a system of payments to jurors, so that poorer citizens could also afford to serve. Pericles is recorded as having said: "We are called a democracy, for the government is in the hands of the many not the few. . . when a citizen is in any way distinguished, he is promoted to the public service, not as a matter of privilege, but as a reward of merit."

◀ Pericles dominated Athenian politics during the time of the city-states' greatest glory, from about 460 B.C.E. until his death from plague in 429 B.C.E.

Cicero (106–43 B.C.E.) addresses the Roman Senate. Cicero was a politician and orator who lived towards the end of the Roman Republic.

ANCIENT ROME

In the sixth century B.C.E., the ancient Romans developed a system of government called a "republic," from *respublica,* Latin for "the thing that belongs to the people." Not a democracy in the Greek sense, their republic nonetheless contained some democratic elements. Executive power was placed in the hands of two consuls (officials) who were elected annually. In an effort to prevent either of them becoming too powerful, they were given the right to veto (reject) each other's decisions. The power of the consuls was further checked by an assembly of patricians (the wealthy ruling class) called the Senate, who served for life. A political struggle between the patricians and the plebeians (ordinary citizens) resulted in the establishment of an Assembly of Tribes, on which all citizens were free to serve. The Assembly could approve or reject certain laws and vote on issues of war and peace. Most political power, however, remained with the consuls and the Senate.

The demands of ruling a vast empire placed strains on the Roman Republic. A power struggle between two consuls eventually led to a civil war. In 45 B.C.E., a military leader, Julius Caesar, took power and ended the republican system of government. By 27 B.C.E., Rome was under the control of a single emperor, with the Senate reduced to a merely advisory body.

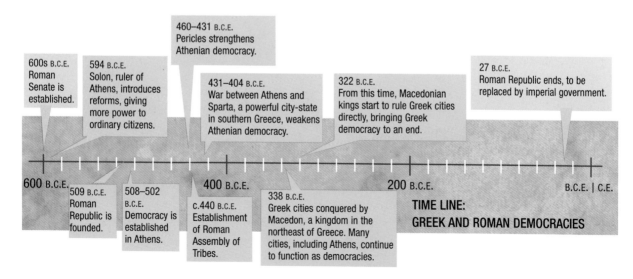

600s B.C.E. Roman Senate is established.

594 B.C.E. Solon, ruler of Athens, introduces reforms, giving more power to ordinary citizens.

460–431 B.C.E. Pericles strengthens Athenian democracy.

431–404 B.C.E. War between Athens and Sparta, a powerful city-state in southern Greece, weakens Athenian democracy.

322 B.C.E. From this time, Macedonian kings start to rule Greek cities directly, bringing Greek democracy to an end.

27 B.C.E. Roman Republic ends, to be replaced by imperial government.

600 B.C.E.

509 B.C.E. Roman Republic is founded.

508–502 B.C.E. Democracy is established in Athens.

c.440 B.C.E. Establishment of Roman Assembly of Tribes.

400 B.C.E.

338 B.C.E. Greek cities conquered by Macedon, a kingdom in the northeast of Greece. Many cities, including Athens, continue to function as democracies.

200 B.C.E.

B.C.E. | C.E.

TIME LINE: GREEK AND ROMAN DEMOCRACIES

▲ This fourteenth-century illustration, showing a noble and the peasants who work his land, gives an idea of the power wielded by the upper classes in feudal society.

FEUDALISM

The Greek and Roman experiments with democracy ended when the Roman Empire replaced the Roman Republic in 27 B.C.E. Democratic government would not be seen again in Europe—or anywhere else—for many centuries. After the Roman Empire fell in the fifth century C.E., Europe became a mass of tribal chiefdoms that slowly evolved into nations run by absolute monarchs. Between the eighth and fourteenth centuries, a system known as feudalism developed. Under feudalism, power rested in the hands of a wealthy élite, at the top of which was the king. In return for access to land, lower social classes had to obey those ranked above them. The Christian church taught that kings had a divine right to rule, which reinforced the existing order.

COUNCILS AND ASSEMBLIES

Despite the effects of feudalism, representative bodies did emerge. Between 600 and 1000 C.E., a local assembly of Viking freemen (but not slaves or women), called a Ting, regularly met in the Trondheim region of Norway to accept or reject laws and settle disputes. By 900 there were similar local assemblies all over Scandinavia. The Vikings, like the Greeks, believed in political equality, at least among free-born men. When Viking settlers arrived in Iceland, they took their political ideas with them, and in 930 founded a national assembly called the Althing—often described as the oldest surviving parliament in Europe. The Althing met for two weeks every summer to pass laws and judge on legal disputes.

In other parts of Europe, kings ruled with absolute authority, yet regularly consulted with councils of bishops and barons. Over time, the power of the councils grew, and they expanded to include not just nobility and clergymen but commoners, known as knights and burghers (townsmen). These councils (or assemblies)—although not at all representative of the wider population of peasants—were the ancestors of today's legislatures. By the mid-fourteenth century, assemblies had been established in several European kingdoms. England's Parliament was the most influential in terms of the future development of democracy. It had two legislative bodies: the king's advisors, known as the House of Lords, and a second chamber, the House of Commons, consisting of knights, burghers, and clergymen.

THE MAGNA CARTA

The Magna Carta (meaning Great Charter), drawn up in 1215, is one of the founding documents of English democracy. It established the principle that the king was not above the law, and that the monarch's powers were restricted by his baronial advisers (and later, Parliament). King John, who ruled England at this time, had made his barons unhappy by raising taxes to fund a war with France in which the English were defeated. The barons reasserted their power by forcing John to sign the Magna Carta. The document stated, for example, that the king could not raise a tax that had not first been approved by them, and that he could not imprison citizens without good reason. Although John later rejected the Magna Carta, future kings reaffirmed it, and it became one of the key documents in the English constitution.

Democratic ideals were also revived at a more local level in the twelfth and thirteenth centuries. Many towns and cities had grown in wealth and importance and had gained political independence. In Italy during the twelfth century, Roman-style republics re-emerged in a number of cities, including Florence, Padua, Pisa, Milan, and Siena. Officials known as *podestà* headed ruling councils, where they combined executive and judicial powers. They were elected annually by male property owners. By the mid-fourteenth century, however,

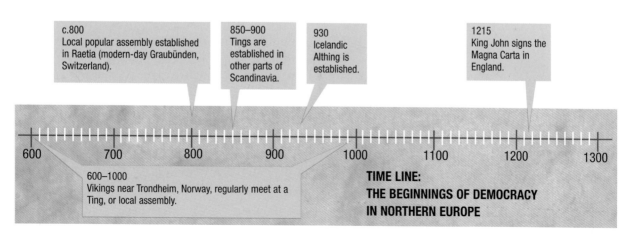

c.800
Local popular assembly established in Raetia (modern-day Graubünden, Switzerland).

850–900
Tings are established in other parts of Scandinavia.

930
Icelandic Althing is established.

1215
King John signs the Magna Carta in England.

600 700 800 900 1000 1100 1200 1300

600–1000
Vikings near Trondheim, Norway, regularly meet at a Ting, or local assembly.

TIME LINE:
THE BEGINNINGS OF DEMOCRACY
IN NORTHERN EUROPE

these republican governments were giving way, once again, to more authoritarian forms of rule.

Cultures outside of Europe, according to some historical evidence, may have practiced democracy in earlier times. For example, in 1520, a group of Native Americans formed an alliance called the Iroquois Confederacy. They adopted the "Great Law of Peace," which acted as a constitution, defining the role of their government and giving guidelines about how nations could resolve disputes and maintain peace. Some historians believe the Iroquois Confederacy influenced the founders of the U.S. Constitution.

THE RISE OF THE BRITISH PARLIAMENT

In the seventeenth century, most European monarchs had regained dominance over their assemblies, and progress towards democracy appeared to go into reverse. The exception to this was England (known, after 1707, as Great Britain), where Parliament became engaged in a

▲ Parliament's victory in the English Civil War did not immediately advance the cause of democracy. Just five years later, Parliament was dissolved (as shown in this picture) and six months later power was handed to the "Lord Protector," Oliver Cromwell, who effectively ruled England as a dictator until his death in 1658.

prolonged power struggle with the crown, or monarch. The result was a victory for Parliament in the English Civil War (1640–1648), and the execution of the king. Although the monarchy was restored in 1660, Parliament held on to most of its newly won powers.

In 1688, another power struggle ended in the defeat and exile of King James II. Parliament secured its central role in the English constitution in 1689 by presenting James' successors, William and Mary, with a Declaration of Rights. This stated that Parliament should meet frequently, that elections should be free and fair, that Members of Parliament should have freedom of speech, and that parliamentary consent was necessary in order to raise taxes and maintain professional armies. England was not yet a democracy, because the monarchy remained a very powerful institution and only males from the upper social classes, a minority of the total population, had the vote—but important democratic principles had been established.

THE AMERICAN REVOLUTION

In the eighteenth century, an intellectual movement known as the Enlightenment spread through Europe. It argued the need for a more rational approach to human affairs and an end to traditional, outdated ideas such as the divine right of kings. Enlightenment thinkers admired Britain's Declaration of Rights and its commitment to freedom of speech.

In the latter part of the century, Britain's colonies in North America became angry that they had to pay taxes to Britain, yet were not represented in its parliament. Some of the colonists decided to fight for their independence. In 1776, one of their leaders, Thomas Jefferson, wrote the Declaration of Independence.

The Declaration of Independence was influenced by the ideas of John Locke and Jean-Jacques Rousseau, Enlightenment philosophers who argued that people should have a say in how their government is run and that governments should protect people's rights to life and liberty. In 1783, American revolutionaries defeated British forces, and Britain had to accept the independence of American colonies which, when the new constitution was agreed upon by the states, became the United States of America.

"We hold these Truths to be self-evident, that all Men are created equal, that they are endowed by their Creator with certain unalienable Rights, that among these are Life, Liberty and the pursuit of Happiness."

The opening words of the Declaration of Independence, 1776.

Thomas Jefferson (1743–1826), a founding father of the United States, who served as the country's third president. ▶

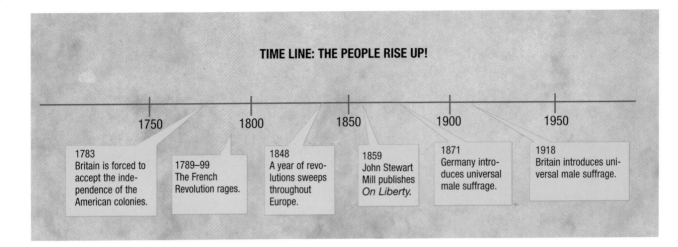

TIME LINE: THE PEOPLE RISE UP!

1750 · 1800 · 1850 · 1900 · 1950

1783
Britain is forced to accept the independence of the American colonies.

1789–99
The French Revolution rages.

1848
A year of revolutions sweeps throughout Europe.

1859
John Stewart Mill publishes *On Liberty*.

1871
Germany introduces universal male suffrage.

1918
Britain introduces universal male suffrage.

The former colonies, now states, did not want to give up all their powers to the new national government. Those in charge of putting together the new constitution therefore gave the country a federal structure. Each state retained its own local government, and the central—or federal—government was given the responsibility of passing and carrying out laws on matters concerning the nation as a whole. The branches of government were made separate from one another to avoid domination by any individual or group. The United States was the world's first modern democracy—although almost two centuries would pass before every person in the country (including African Americans and women) could fully benefit from the rights and freedoms of its constitution.

During the nineteenth century, increasing numbers of countries were encouraged to embrace democracy by the strong examples of Great Britain, the United States, and France. By the end of the century, almost all Western European countries, as well as Canada, Australia, and New Zealand, had developed democratic representative legislatures and constitutional monarchies.

UNIVERSAL MALE SUFFRAGE

Social changes in the nineteenth century put pressure on governments to widen the vote (also known as the franchise, or suffrage) beyond a minority of men. The Industrial Revolution, which swept through Europe and the United States during this period, created a large middle class, who

THE FRENCH REVOLUTION

The Enlightenment, and the example of the American Revolution, inspired radicals in France to overthrow their monarch in 1789. They drafted a "Declaration of the Rights of Man," which claimed that the source of all sovereignty lies with the nation. Despite this, the revolutionaries believed in retaining a monarch, but limiting his or her powers by a constitution. However, a more extreme group took control of France in 1793, leading to the execution of the king, Louis XVI, and many French aristocrats. France returned to authoritarian rule under Napoleon Bonaparte, who was in power between 1799 and 1815, yet the ideas associated with the French Revolution would prove very influential in the long term.

◀ The execution of King Louis XVI during the French Revolution. The revolution took the king completely by surprise. On the day it started, he wrote in his diary: "Rien" ("Nothing happened").

try to introduce universal male suffrage, quickly followed by France. By the 1930s, universal male suffrage—the right to vote— had been achieved throughout the continent.

SLAVERY

By the mid-nineteenth century in the United States, all white men had been given the right to vote. The nation's commitment to democracy and political equality was undermined, however, by the continued existence of slavery in its southern states. Slaves of African descent had been working on plantations in

wished for political representation to go with their new-found prosperity. Industrialization also created a massive urban working class of factory laborers, who gradually began to realize they could exert considerable power when they joined forces with one another. They, too, wished for a say in running their country. The extension of suffrage to all men became an important goal for many political activists during the nineteenth century.

In Britain, the Reform Acts of 1832, 1867, and 1884 enfranchised the middle class and large parts of the urban and rural working class. In 1871, Germany became the first European coun-

the South since the mid-seventeenth century, and by the early 1800s there were increasing calls from the northern states to abolish slavery. Slavery was one of the main causes of the civil war between the South and the North in the 1860s, which the South lost. In 1866, slavery was outlawed in the United States, but African Americans would not achieve political equality for another hundred years.

WOMEN'S STRUGGLE FOR THE VOTE

Most of the struggles to extend voting rights during the nineteenth century ignored the case of women, the last group to get the vote. The first demands for women's suffrage came from the United States in the mid-nineteenth century, and the first state to enfranchise women was Wyoming, in 1869. Several other states followed as women demonstrated, were arrested for their activities on behalf of women's suffrage, and worked for their rights as part of a worldwide civil rights movement—the largest the world had ever known. In the end, nationwide change could only be achieved by the Nineteenth Amendment to the U.S. Constitution, called the Susan B. Anthony Amendment, which finally passed in 1920. Before that, in 1893, New Zealand became the first country to offer women the vote, followed by Australia in 1902.

In Britain, the women's suffrage movement was launched in 1903. The suffragettes, as they were known, resorted to increasingly militant activities to attract publicity for their cause. They used methods such as chaining themselves to railings and breaking shop windows in order to get arrested. In 1928, British women finally achieved political equality with men.

EMMELINE PANKHURST
As a founder of the Women's Social and Political Union, Emmeline Pankhurst (1857–1928) was one of the leading campaigners for women's suffrage in Britain between 1903 and 1914. Her daughters, Christabel and Sylvia, were also active in the movement. Emmeline's law-breaking tactics led to her imprisonment on several occasions. While in prison, she went on hunger strike and was force-fed by prison officers. Pankhurst died in 1928, having achieved her main goal: the right of British women to vote.

◀ On June 5, 1915, 20,000 Danish suffragettes marched to the Amalienborg Palace in Copenhagen to witness the signing of a new constitution, giving women the right to vote in Denmark. It marked the end of a twenty-seven-year struggle.

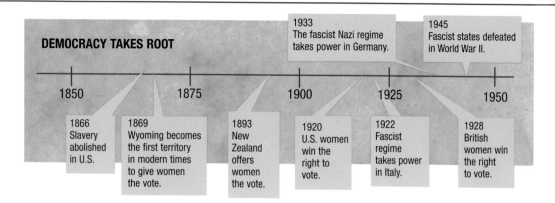

DEMOCRACY TAKES ROOT

1850   1875   1900   1925   1950

1933
The fascist Nazi regime takes power in Germany.

1945
Fascist states defeated in World War II.

1866
Slavery abolished in U.S.

1869
Wyoming becomes the first territory in modern times to give women the vote.

1893
New Zealand offers women the vote.

1920
U.S. women win the right to vote.

1922
Fascist regime takes power in Italy.

1928
British women win the right to vote.

THE FASCIST THREAT

By the early twentieth century, democracy had become the established form of government in most Western countries. It faced severe challenges, however, from strongly authoritarian, antidemocratic systems of government. One such system was fascism. Fascists tend to believe in the superiority of their nation and, often, their race.

Fascist movements sprang up in various parts of Europe in the 1920s and 1930s, overthrowing democratic governments in Germany, Italy, and Spain. They arose partly as a reaction to democracy, which fascists saw as weak and compromising. Fascism was destroyed as a significant political force when the Allies defeated Germany and Italy during World War II.

Italian fascist guards march over a bridge in Venice, Italy, in June 1934. Part of the appeal of fascism for many people was that it conveyed a strong sense of group identity and discipline. ▼

THE CHALLENGE OF COMMUNISM

Political parties representing the working classes emerged in the late nineteenth and early twentieth centuries as socialist and communist parties worked to obtain better conditions for workers. Communists hoped to overturn the dominant economic system, known as capitalism, in which private owners control trade and industry for profit. They wished to replace capitalism with a new system in which wealth and property are controlled by the state.

Communism, with its authoritarian tendencies, threatened the basic principles of democracy—although its supporters argued that political equality was unlikely to be achieved without economic equality, and this could only occur if all wealth was controlled by the state. Communism also tried to undermine national identity by calling upon workers of all countries to unite in a common struggle.

During the twentieth century, a number of countries turned communist. Most of these countries, such as Russia and China, had no democratic traditions in place. These states claimed to be more democratic than capitalist states, because they removed the privileges of wealth. In practice, communism proved extremely undemocratic, with its centralization of economic and political power, leaving no room for the will of the people. Neverthelesss, Communist regimes inspired supporters in the West to try to overthrow democratic capitalist governments. By the 1990s, however, the Soviet Union's collapse and increased capitalism in China made communism seem to be a spent force, no longer a threat to democracy.

THE TRIUMPH OF DEMOCRACY

With the defeat of fascism and successful struggles for freedom from European colonial domination, the second half of the twentieth century saw democratic progress in various parts of the world. By 1950, twenty-two

"The first thing to do to . . . enable the working people to enjoy democracy in practice is to deprive the exploiters of all the public and sumptuous private buildings, to give to the working people leisure, and to see to it that their freedom of assembly is protected by armed workers, not by heirs of the nobility or capitalist officers in command of downtrodden soldiers. . . . Genuine democracy . . . is unrealizable unless this aim is achieved."

Vladimir Ilyich Lenin, communist leader of the Soviet Union, 1919.

▲ A communist rally in 1920s Berlin, Germany. During the early decades of the twentieth century, it appeared to many people that communism offered hope for the future.

democracies existed, accounting for 31 percent of the world's population, and a further twenty-one states enjoyed some elements of democracy.

By the mid-1960s, democracy could at last be enjoyed by all U.S. citizens. Until that time, many African Americans in the South had been discriminated against. In spite of the Fifteenth Amendment to the U.S. Constitution (which guaranteed all men, regardless of race, color, or previous condition of servitude, the right to vote) they were denied voting rights and forced to live as second-class citizens. Opponents of this injustice formed the Civil Rights Movement and put pressure on the federal government to pass the 1964 Civil Rights Act to end racial segregation in schools and public places. With this struggle, African Americans gained political equality.

In the 1990s, communism's collapse brought democracy to Russia and Eastern Europe. Pro-democracy movements in Africa triumphed in Nigeria, Togo, Tanzania, Malawi, and South Africa. Countries in Asia and South America also gained increased democracy.

▲ A protester is attacked by a police dog during a civil rights demonstration in the United States in the 1950s.

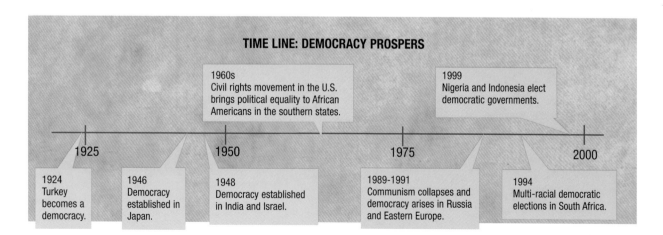

TIME LINE: DEMOCRACY PROSPERS

1960s
Civil rights movement in the U.S. brings political equality to African Americans in the southern states.

1999
Nigeria and Indonesia elect democratic governments.

1925   1950   1975   2000

1924
Turkey becomes a democracy.

1946
Democracy established in Japan.

1948
Democracy established in India and Israel.

1989-1991
Communism collapses and democracy arises in Russia and Eastern Europe.

1994
Multi-racial democratic elections in South Africa.

CHAPTER THREE
MODERN DEMOCRACY IN ACTION

Each modern democratic country has its own unique features and ways of operating. All democracies, however, have certain basic elements in common. These include the three branches of government: the executive, legislative, and judiciary.

EXECUTIVES

The executive has two functions: to formulate policies, and to put those policies into action. The first function is carried out by politicians—the chief executive (the prime minister or president) and the cabinet—those they have appointed to advise and help them. The second is carried out by a permanent, non-political staff of professionals, known as the civil service.

In the latter half of the twentieth century, people in the developed world began to demand more from the state in terms of health care, education, and other social services. At the same time, the Cold War (1945–1990) led to more spending on military and security operations. A larger executive branch was required to deal with all these demands. Western countries have therefore developed vast civil services. This enormous array of services has made it harder for the politicians—the chief executive and the cabinet—to be involved in every aspect of policy. Consequently, a great deal of delegation (handing over of certain responsibilities) now occurs, and more power has been placed in the hands of unelected civil servants. This trend has also made it much more difficult for the legislative branch to act as an effective check on executive power.

Chief executives tend to become more involved in the areas of foreign policy and homeland security, where urgent or secret action is often required. When a national crisis occurs, such as the terrorist attacks on the United States on September 11, 2001, a decisive response is

THE POWER OF THE PRESIDENCY

The people who devised the U.S. Constitution realized the country needed a strong chief executive — especially in the area of foreign policy. They were careful, however, also to build in safeguards so that these powers could not be abused. For example, the president is commander-in-chief of the armed forces, but only Congress has the power to declare war. The president can make appointments to the cabinet and the Supreme Court, and can make treaties with other countries, but only with Congressional approval. The president can make policy, but only Congress can raise taxes and approve budgets to pay for these policies. Finally, Congress can impeach a president if he has committed a crime or abused his powers.

China's National People's Congress (NPC) meets once a year in March. Although the NPC's powers have increased since the mid-1980s, China continues to be controlled by the unelected leaders of the Communist Party. ▶

needed. In situations such as this, the chief executive may wish to enact policies (such as the war on terror and the attack on Afghanistan) with minimal consultation with other parts of government.

At such times, the legislature may have less opportunity to scrutinize executive actions. Legally, however, the U.S. Congress must give consent before the president can order U.S. troops to invade a foreign country, as it did, with limitations, in the war on the Taliban in Afghanistan.

LEGISLATURES

Legislative assemblies pass and repeal (cancel) laws and act as a check on the executive. In China, which is not a democracy, the National People's Congress has nearly 3,000 delegates. It meets infrequently and has little power or independence. In contrast, the U.S. Congress is a for-

◀ U.S. troops search for Taliban terrorists in Afghanistan in 2002. The U.S. Congress gave president George W. Bush limited authorization (through the War Powers Act) to send troops in the U.S.-led coalition attack, which began in October 2001.

midable institution that can block and amend legislation that comes from the executive (the president). It can even come up with proposals of its own.

Legislatures oversee the executive in various ways. Many have powerful committees, separate from the main assembly, where they scrutinize legislation and propose amendments, approve budgets, or sometimes conduct investigations into possible abuses of executive power. Another form of control, exercised by the British Parliament, is Question Time, in which members of Parliament regularly question the executive (Prime Minister) on the floor of the legislature. In presidential systems, the assembly must usually approve the appointments of the executive, such as senior politicians and judges.

Most modern legislatures have two chambers (assemblies) providing two forms of representation and also acting as a brake or check on each other. Second chambers are often appointed, or elected indirectly, and they are usually much weaker than first chambers. An exception to this is the U.S. Senate, whose senators are elected directly on a state-by-state basis. The Senate is equal in power to the first chamber, the House of Representatives.

> *"The great virtue of a strong legislature is not what it can do, but what it can prevent."*
>
> U.S. Senator J. W. Fulbright (1905–1995) .

JUDICIARIES

Judiciaries, or the courts, act as an important check on the executive and legislative branches of government. Their job is to interpret the constitution and the law as they apply to individual cases. In the United States, the Supreme Court has made some momentous decisions in its history. In Brown versus the Board of Education (1954), the court outlawed school segregation (and effectively all racial segregation) in the United States. The Roe versus Wade case (1973) resulted in the legalization of women's right to choose an abortion.

POLITICAL PARTIES

Political parties perform an important function in democracies. They bring together broad coalitions of people who alone would have little chance of getting their voices heard. They help set out the choices for voters, who can tell broadly what a candidate's political views are by the party he or she belongs to. They also provide governments with a relatively stable block of political supporters to help them carry out their policies once in power. Some parties, such as the Democratic Party in the United States, have managed at some points to embrace a very wide range of views, including those of southern conservatives and northern liberals. Other parties, such as the Green parties of Europe, focus on policies to do with the environment and therefore have more specific concerns.

In a parliamentary system, if the government fails on an important vote, that government "falls." The Prime Minister and cabinet resign. If no other leader manages to form a government, Parliament is "dissolved" and a new election must be held.

In Britain, the main parties—Labour and Conservative—are very powerful. Under the government of Tony Blair, Labour's huge majority in the House of Commons (since 1997) has almost guaranteed that legislation introduced by his government will be passed. In this way, the executive tends to dominate the legislature. The very size of the majority, however, has encouraged rebellions by some Labour MPs, who in this case feel they can register their opposition to certain policies without risking the downfall of the government.

ELECTORAL SYSTEMS

There are two main kinds of systems by which assemblies are elected in today's democracies. One of these is "first-past-the-post." Under this sys-

▲ George W. Bush celebrates his nomination for president at the Republican National Convention in 2000.

tem, the country is divided into electoral districts, or constituencies, and only one candidate—the one who attracts the most votes—is elected from each constituency. The other system, which takes various forms, is known as proportional representation (PR). Under PR systems, several of the most popular candidates can be elected from each constituency.

First-past-the-post favors larger, more established parties, who are likely to have a greater number of outright winners. This system is liable to produce a stronger, more stable government. Assemblies elected by PR tend to reflect the pattern of votes cast. PR is therefore often regarded as more democratic.

The disadvantage of PR is that by giving representation to many parties it can create weak, divided government. In Italy, between 1947 and

THE ELECTORAL COLLEGE

In the United States, the president is not elected directly. The people of each state send representatives to an electoral college to vote on their behalf. Each state is allocated a certain number of representatives depending on the size of its population. For example, Alaska, which has a small population, sends three electors to the electoral college, while California, with a large population, sends 55. The winning candidate in a state wins the votes of all that state's electors at the electoral college. This winner-takes-all system can produce some unexpected outcomes. In the 2000 election, more Americans voted for the Demo-cratic candidate, Al Gore, but because his Republican opponent, George W. Bush, had a majority in the electoral college, Bush became president. This occurred only after a highly controversial legal battle, fought in part because the state of Florida was found to have used flawed voting equipment. The popular votes (and thus the electoral college votes) were therefore legally contested and required a decision from the U.S. Supreme Court. Electoral college victories also occurred in 1876 and 1888, but they did not require intervention by the Supreme Court.

FUNDRAISING ON THE INTERNET

In the United States, the 2003–2004 contest to decide on the Democratic candidate for president was remarkable for a technological reason. It was the first time the power of the Internet had been used so effectively in support of a national political campaign. Candidate Howard Dean's campaign created a vast network of support— and raised a huge amount of money—simply through spreading the word on a web site called *Meetup.com*. Dean's Internet campaign captured world attention because it appeared to put political power back in the hands of ordinary people. The average donation from Dean's supporters was just $77, yet the sheer number of donors brought him a total of $25 million in just six months. In contrast, most modern political campaigns rely on rich donors, leaving candidates feeling obliged to support powerful interest groups once elected. Despite his fundraising success, Dean's campaign was not successful enough during the primary elections to win the Democratic nomination for president.

▲ Italian premier Silvio Berlusconi after his election victory in March 1994. His government lasted just seven months. Berlusconi returned as leader in 2001, and in 2004 his government became the longest-lasting government to serve in Italy since 1946.

1996, thanks to its PR system, governments lasted an average of just six months. With around fourteen parties represented in parliament, government found it hard to agree on any issue. New Zealand, by contrast, had just two parties in its assembly, and very stable governments, until the introduction of PR in 1996.

PRESSURE GROUPS

Pressure groups operate in all democracies. They are organizations of people who work to promote a particular interest or concern, by lobbying governments and raising public awareness through various kinds of campaigns. Some pressure groups— for example, trade unions or professional associa-

tions—have established links with government and easy and regular access to representatives and civil servants. Governments appreciate these links with groups that can give them technical advice when formulating policies.

Other groups fighting for minority causes, or politically controversial issues, such as the environment, animal rights, or anti-abortion, do not enjoy such levels of access. They must therefore find alternative ways of promoting themselves and exerting pressure. One method is to organize national campaigns with the help of the media.

Another approach, often taken by business interest groups, is to try to influence politicians by offering donations to their re-election campaigns. Many have criticized this practice as unde-mocratic, since it means that some candidates, par-ticularly those from established parties, have far more to spend on their campaigns than others. In 2001, to help balance this, the U.S. government passed the Bipartisan Campaign Reform Act, which banned unlimited contributions to political parties from large businesses, unions, and individuals.

THE MEDIA AND DEMOCRACY

Since 1945, the executive has expanded greatly, making it harder for elected representatives to monitor the activities of government. This role has increasingly been taken up by the free press.

The media's investigative journalists have uncov-ered many instances of political corruption and abuse of power. The most famous example was the Watergate scandal. In 1972, burglars connected to the re-election committee of President Nixon (a Republican), broke into the Democratic National Committee headquarters in the Watergate building in Washington, D.C. They tapped the phones and photographed documents. Two reporters from the *Washington Post* newspaper discovered that Nixon had approved payments to the burglars in exchange for their silence. Nixon had also tried to get government agencies to help cover up the crime. The journalists' reports in the

Washington Post reporters Carl Bernstein (in chair) and Bob Woodward, who uncovered the Watergate scandal, watch President Nixon announce the resignation, in April 1973, of the Attorney General and several members of the White House staff who were involved in Watergate. Nixon himself resigned fifteen months later. ▼

Washington Post eventually caused Nixon to resign or face impeachment proceedings. He chose to resign.

In addition to providing a check on governmental power and misdeeds, the media has also become a powerful influence on public opinion, especially during elections. In most democracies,

> "Freedom of the press affords the public one of the best means of discovering and forming an opinion of the ideas and attitudes of their political leaders ... it thus enables everyone to participate in the free political debate which is at the very core of the concept of a democratic society."
>
> From a judgement made by the European Court of Human Rights on 25 June 1992.

newspapers tend to have a strong political bias, and it is possible that in close contests they can actually help swing election results toward one party or another. This may have been the case in the 1992 British general election, when fourteen of the seventeen national newspapers supported the Conservative Party, and the unfavored Conservatives won.

Television news reporting tends to be more politically neutral, although in France there are regular accusations of pro-government bias. In the United States, many people felt that Fox News was too uncritical of the U.S. government in its reporting of the 2003 Iraq War, while the BBC was accused of anti-government bias by the British government in its coverage of the same war.

Television news tends to be superficial, often emphasizing personalities and images more than in-depth analysis. This approach has encouraged modern politics to grow more image conscious. Party conferences are often now stage-managed media events. Election candidates look for "photo opportunities." Rather than make long, thoughtful speeches, politicians tend to offer short, media-friendly statements, or "sound bites." This has led some to believe the media has trivialized politics.

◀ Journalists in Paris at a press conference held by French president Jacques Chirac. Politicians and the media have a complex relationship. They depend on one another to some extent, and so, in most cases, neither can afford to be too hostile.

CHAPTER FOUR

THE STRUGGLE FOR DEMOCRACY

While most developed countries now enjoy the benefits of democracy and the rights and freedoms that come with it, many countries in the developing world continue to live under autocratic regimes (governments with unlimited power). Fighting this trend are some remarkable countries that have either recently achieved democracy or are currently struggling toward it.

SOUTH AFRICA

The state of South Africa was founded in 1910. Its minority white population of British and Dutch descent ruled over a much larger population of blacks, Asians, and people of mixed race. The white rulers wanted to keep their privileged position, so they introduced a system of laws, known as apartheid, intended to separate whites from nonwhites. The nonwhites were denied political rights: They were not allowed to vote and their movements were severely restricted.

In 1912, an organization called the African National Congress (ANC) was formed to campaign for equal rights for black people. In 1948, the white-only National Party came to power. Under its rule the apartheid system was extended further. Black people were forced to live in "homelands" (poor rural areas) and travel miles to work every day. Buses, parks, beaches, and many other public areas were segregated along racial lines. The activities of the ANC were violently repressed by the National Party in government, and many of its leaders were imprisoned.

▲ South Africa's apartheid system (seen operating here in 1989) created a privileged lifestyle for the minority white population, while denying nonwhites the most basic human rights.

Opposition bravely continued, however, while the government used increasingly brutal repression, arousing international condemnation. As more and more of the world's nations refused to do business with South Africa, it began to feel the effects of political and economic isolation. Finally, in the late 1980s, the country's leadership bowed to pressure and announced the removal of most apartheid laws. The ANC was recognized as a valid political party, and its leaders were freed in 1990.

After four years of negotiations between the ANC, the government, and other groups, South Africa held its first multiracial elections. The ANC emerged as the clear winner, and its leader, Nelson Mandela, became the country's first black president. The National Party, winning more than twenty seats in the election, was allowed representation in the cabinet, easing white fears about the new, predominantly black government.

The government faced enormous challenges to overcome the bitter legacy of apartheid and to restore trust between the different ethnic groups of South Africa. In 1996, a Truth and Reconciliation Commission was set up to encourage people to talk about past injustices and help heal the country's divisions. For many, this proved a painful but important experience.

"I queued [lined up] from nine in the morning until six at night—but if I had to, I would have stayed out until morning. I was very excited. I thought now things would happen. Not too much, but somewhat. A child doesn't just get up and walk. He starts sitting, then crawling, and then walking and talking. You have to give him a chance. So I think we need to give the new government a chance."

Maria Zulu, a South African woman, recalls election day in 1994.

Between April 26 and 29, 1994, around twenty million black South Africans lined up outside polling stations for a chance to vote for the first time in their lives. ▶

Braks ruit Garage

VOTE HERE   VOUTA MONA
STEM HIER   VOTA LAPHA

In 1999, the ANC secured a second election victory. Some worried that the ANC's monopoly of power endangered democracy, but this is unlikely, as South Africa has a strong democratic constitution with powerful opposition parties.

MYANMAR

The country of Myanmar (also known as Burma) in Southeast Asia has been ruled by a military dictatorship since 1962. In 1988, the army violently put down an uprising of students and workers and killed thousands of unarmed protesters. The slaughter prompted Aung San Suu Kyi, the daughter of a former leader of Myanmar, to speak out against the regime, and she founded a nonviolent movement for democracy and human rights, the National League for Democracy (NLD).

When multi-party elections were allowed in 1990, Aung San Suu Kyi was already under house arrest (not allowed to leave her home). Nevertheless, she led the NLD to a landslide victory, winning 80 percent of contested parliamentary seats. The result was ignored by the regime, and they continued to persecute the NLD.

Aung San Suu Kyi's courageous fight for democracy brought her worldwide admiration, and in 1991 she won the Nobel Peace Prize. She was released in 1995, but placed once more under house arrest in February 2003, where she remains. Myanmar remains firmly under authoritarian rule. Numerous human rights abuses, including the forcible relocation of civilians and widespread use of forced labor have occurred, but the government-controlled media has been unable to report these issues.

EASTERN EUROPE

During the 1980s, the leader of the USSR, Mikhail Gorbachev, began to reform the Soviet political system, making it more open and democratic. He encouraged many of the Soviet-controlled states of Eastern Europe to do the same. In 1989, the Hungarian parliament legalized opposition parties and announced multi-party elections. It also opened its border with noncommunist Austria.

Later that year, Poland also permitted opposition parties and announced elections. In November 1989, the East German government was pressured into opening the Berlin Wall, which had divided the city since 1961, and had been a hated symbol of the Cold War. The uprising quickly spread to Bulgaria, Czechoslovakia, and Romania. Unpopular communist leaders were overthrown, and democratic elec-

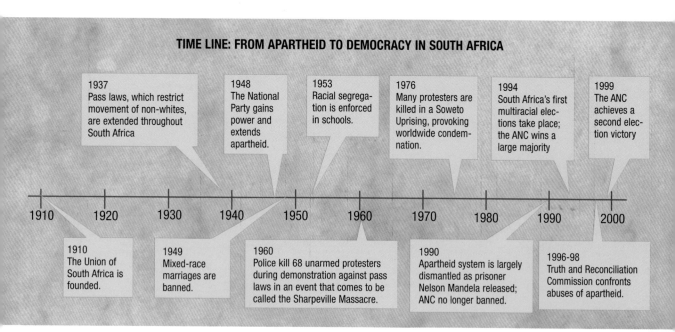

TIME LINE: FROM APARTHEID TO DEMOCRACY IN SOUTH AFRICA

1937
Pass laws, which restrict movement of non-whites, are extended throughout South Africa

1948
The National Party gains power and extends apartheid.

1953
Racial segregation is enforced in schools.

1976
Many protesters are killed in a Soweto Uprising, provoking worldwide condemnation.

1994
South Africa's first multiracial elections take place; the ANC wins a large majority

1999
The ANC achieves a second election victory

1910 1920 1930 1940 1950 1960 1970 1980 1990 2000

1910
The Union of South Africa is founded.

1949
Mixed-race marriages are banned.

1960
Police kill 68 unarmed protesters during demonstration against pass laws in an event that comes to be called the Sharpeville Massacre.

1990
Apartheid system is largely dismantled as prisoner Nelson Mandela released; ANC no longer banned.

1996-98
Truth and Reconciliation Commission confronts abuses of apartheid.

◄ On one unforgettable night, November 9, 1989, thousands of East Berliners poured unopposed over the wall that had divided their city for 28 years.

tions were called. Change occurred at an astonishing pace, and by 1990, virtually the whole of Eastern Europe was democratic.

Since the heady days of 1989, most Eastern European countries have adapted well to democracy and have remained fairly stable, politically and economically. East and West Germany reunified in 1994, and in 2004, several other Eastern European countries were admitted into the European Union (EU) —an economic and political alliance of Western Europe. Russia has struggled with choices between candidates who favor democracy and others who overtly or covertly promise to be dictators.

CHINA

Gorbachev's reforms also inspired a prodemocracy movement in communist China. In April 1989, tens of thousands of students and other demonstrators began gathering in public areas in many of China's cities, demanding democratic reforms. The focus of the movement was Tiananmen Square in the capital, Beijing, where around 100,000 gathered. A statue named the "Goddess of Democracy" was erected there. By mid-May, the authorities had virtually lost control of Beijing, which had been occupied by around a million protesters. On June 3, the government sent

December 7, 1988
Gorbachev offers "freedom of choice" in Eastern Europe.

January 1989
Hungary legalizes opposition parties and announces elections.

April 5, 1989
Poland legalizes opposition parties and announces elections.

November 9, 1989
Berlin Wall opens East and West Germany.

December 22, 1989
Downfall of communism in Romania.

October 3, 1990
East and West Germany reunited.

| Dec 88 | Mar 89 | June 89 | Sept 89 | Dec 89 | Mar 90 | June 90 |

May 1989
Border opened between Hungary and Austria.

June 1989
Solidarity (the main Polish opposition party) wins the election over communists.

November 10, 1989
Downfall of communism in Bulgaria.

**TIME LINE:
DEMOCRACY COMES TO EASTERN EUROPE**

SAAD EDDIN IBRAHIM

Saad Eddin Ibrahim (1939–) is a renowned campaigner for democracy and civil rights in Egypt. In 1988, he founded the Ibn Khaldun Center for Development Studies in Cairo, an institute that monitors Egyptian elections and strives to educate voters about democracy. Ibrahim was critical of irregularities in the Egyptian elections of 1990 and 1995. He was arrested in 2000, and thus prevented from monitoring the 2000 elections. Ibrahim was tried on several charges, including "deliberately disseminating [spreading] false information abroad harmful to Egypt's interests." He was sentenced to seven years in prison, but in March 2003, he was cleared of all charges and released.

in troops, who shot and killed hundreds of demonstrators and arrested thousands more. Within days, the short-lived democratic movement in China, televised around the world, was brutally suppressed.

IRAQ

The Middle Eastern nation of Iraq suffered under the brutal regime of Saddam Hussein from 1979 until 2003, when it was overthrown by a military coalition led by the United States. The coalition established a provisional authority over the country that was replaced by an Iraqi interim government on June 28, 2004, with the goal of preparing the way for nationwide elections, which took place on January 30, 2005. Shiites won a majority in this election and may work to create an Islamic theocracy, which could ban future democratic elections. Iraq is composed of peoples of very different ethnic and religious backgrounds, including Kurds and Sunni and Shiite Muslims. It remains to be seen whether this experiment in imposing democracy on a state with little tradition of this form of government will work.

▲ The Goddess of Democracy, a 33-foot- (10-meter-) high statue inspired by the Statue of Liberty, was created during the Tiananmen Square protests and erected there on May 30, 1989. It was destroyed by Chinese troops during the June 3 massacre.

CHAPTER FIVE

PROBLEMS AND CHALLENGES

Democracy faces many challenges in the modern world—perhaps most of all in the countries where it is long established. Where people are accustomed to the rights and freedoms of democratic rule, they are more likely to take these things for granted. It is easy to forget how recently democracy was achieved in the Western world and how easily democratic countries can slip back into authoritarianism—as happened in Germany, Italy, and Spain in the 1920s and 1930s.

PUBLIC APATHY AND PROTEST

Another problem is the influence of the modern media. Although they have helped people to become more informed about politics, some have argued the media have also contributed to a general lowering of public trust in politicians. Modern political journalists seldom trust the words and deeds of politicians. Skepticism can be a sign of a healthy democracy, but, if taken too far, it can encourage widespread distrust of a country's leaders.

Politicians have tried to protect themselves from media attacks by being more careful about their appearance and the way they speak, even to the point of hiring image consultants and voice coaches. Instead of suggesting long-term solutions to problems, which may lack electoral appeal, they often try to win favorable coverage by offering glib sound bites on the issues of the day. Today's political leaders have teams of advisers and spokespersons, known as "spin doctors." The job of spin doctors is to manipulate news stories that may be harmful to the leader or party, in order to minimize the damage, or even turn them to advantage.

◄ British prime minister Tony Blair following his election victory in 1997. His government has been accused of using media manipulation and spin in the presentation of news stories.

▲ In certain U.S. states, such as Pennsylvania, Virginia, North Carolina, and Florida, many people can now register to vote via the Internet—part of a move toward encouraging higher turnouts by making voting more convenient.

"Democracy is supposed to give you the illusion of choice, like Painkiller X and Painkiller Y. But they're both just aspirin."

In a 1982 interview, Gore Vidal, commentator and novelist, cynically suggests that the political choices open to ordinary people are very limited—even in a democracy.

For example, in November 2001, when President Bush was concerned about media criticism of the war on terror, he appointed Charlotte Beers, a former advertising executive, to "sell" the U.S. administration's case more effectively.

The era of spin and sound bite has deepened the distrust of the political system for ordinary people. In the 1950s and 1960s, 75 percent of Americans trusted their political leaders. By the early 2000s, that figure had slumped to 32 percent. Increasingly people feel that politicians are becoming more self-serving and no longer respond to the needs of ordinary voters. This public cynicism is reflected in lower turnouts at elections. In France, for example, the percentage of people who vote in parliamentary elections fell from 74 percent in 1945 to below 60 percent in 1997.

Some steps have been taken by governments to try to encourage more people to vote. To raise turnout, many countries are investigating the possibilities of making voting easier. Internet voting already exists in some U.S. states, and Germany, Sweden, and the Irish Republic are all considering the introduction of some form of electronic voting for future elections. The UK government is looking into the possibilities of mobile phone voting.

Even if these efforts are successful and more people are persuaded to vote, it may not necessarily benefit the established parties. In recent years, public disillusionment has led to a rise in protest votes, with many electors opting for candidates who are independent of main political parties. In the 1997 UK general election, independent candidate Martin Bell captured what was thought to be a safe Conservative seat. In the U.S. presidential elections of 2000, Green Party candidate Ralph Nader attracted two million votes, despite lacking the funds or TV exposure of his rivals.

Many no longer believe that the normal democratic processes—voting and lobbying, for example —have any real effect. Since the mid-1990s, this feeling has led to a surge in popular protests and demonstrations. In 1999 and 2000, large-scale demonstrations erupted in a number of cities over the insistence by the World Bank that developing countries repay their debts. And in February 2003, millions of people took to the streets in sixty different countries, including the United States, in a global protest against the U.S.-initiated war in Iraq.

THREATS TO THE NATION-STATE

Democracy in its modern form emerged in the nation-states of Europe, the United States, and elsewhere, and people's democratic rights and freedoms are contained within—and protected by—the constitutions of those states. Any threat to the sov-

In January 2003, tens of thousands demonstrated against the war in Iraq on the Mall in Washington, D.C. Similar demonstrations took place in countries around the world, including Japan, Russia, Pakistan, Germany, and the UK. ▼

ereignty of the nation-state is therefore perceived by many as a danger to democracy itself.

One such threat, according to some, is the European Union. With its own economic and social policy and currency, the beginnings of a foreign policy, and even a planned constitution, the EU is in many ways beginning to resemble a state in its own right. Most European citizens, however, still identify with their national governments, and feel far removed from the EU government, particularly its unelected executive.

Nations are further constrained by international treaties and obligations, agreed between members of institutions such as the International Monetary Fund, the International Court, and the United Nations. These bodies may act according to the will of member nations, but their leaders are not directly elected, and their decisions do not necessarily reflect international public opinion. These institutions could therefore potentially threaten democracy in some ways.

There is at the same time a trend toward devolving (handing down) power from central to regional authorities, further eroding the powers of national governments. In Spain, regional assemblies in Catalonia, Galicia, and the Basque region have been given additional powers, and assemblies have also been established in the UK in, for example, Scotland and Wales.

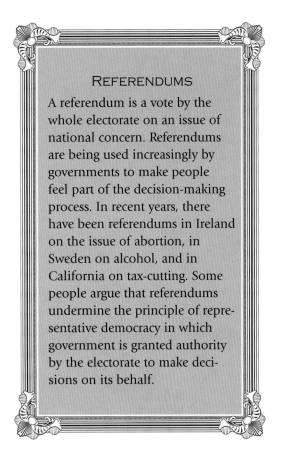

REFERENDUMS

A referendum is a vote by the whole electorate on an issue of national concern. Referendums are being used increasingly by governments to make people feel part of the decision-making process. In recent years, there have been referendums in Ireland on the issue of abortion, in Sweden on alcohol, and in California on tax-cutting. Some people argue that referendums undermine the principle of representative democracy in which government is granted authority by the electorate to make decisions on its behalf.

TNCs AND GLOBALIZATION

The sovereignty of nation-states is further challenged by the rise of transnational corporations (TNCs). These enormous private companies are accountable only to their shareholders, and their primary concern is not the public interest but to make as much money as possible. Yet many are far richer and more powerful in the economic sphere than some smaller nations: The sales of the world's top ten TNCs are greater than the combined GDP (gross domestic product—the total value of all goods and services produced during a year) of southern Africa and South Asia.

TNCs have benefited from a process known as globalization—the development of an integrated global economy based on the free flow of capital around the world. Globalization enables TNCs to lower their costs by exploiting cheap foreign labor markets.

By switching resources from country to country, they can cause poverty and unemployment in the regions they abandon, and elected governments can do very little about it. TNCs and other private companies are even beginning to extend their control into areas traditionally the responsibility of government, such as the provision of electricity, water, and health services. In South Africa, for example, private security companies have taken over the role of policing in many communities.

DOMINATION BY A MAJORITY

In most modern democracies, government policy is usually the result of negotiation between competing minority interests. For example, the competing interests may be business and labor, the security services and civil liberties

▲ More than 20,000 anti-globalization protesters marched through New York City in February 2002, to protest against the World Economic Forum—a gathering of the heads of the world's major corporations—being held there.

groups, religious groups and social liberals, or different ethnic or religious communities. One minority rarely dominates these debates, and a balance of different opinions usually, prevails. In a true democracy, minorities' political rights are protected by a variety of legal safeguards.

In certain divided societies, however, the interests and political rights of a minority can be threatened or ignored by a dominant group, particularly where there is ethnic or religious conflict. Israel is a democracy, and yet Palestinian Arabs living there are often made to feel like second-class citizens. They suffer as an ethnic minority living alongside a much larger population of Jews, many of whom regard them with distrust, given the Palestinians' bloody history of terrorism and fight for an independent Palestinian state. Northern Ireland, with its Protestant majority and Catholic minority, faces a similar situation.

TERRORISM

One of the biggest challenges facing modern democracies—and countries moving towards democracy—is how to deal with terrorism. Terrorism is the use of violence against people and governments in order to achieve political goals. Nondemocratic regimes can deal with terrorism ruthlessly without fear of what effect this might have on public opinion. For example, in 2001, China launched a crackdown against Muslim "terrorists" who wish to have their own Islamic state in western China. Thousands were arrested and held without charge, and the right of Muslims to practice their religion has been limited.

Liberal democracies, however, must tread more carefully: They have to seek a balance between dealing with a terrorist threat and preserving people's rights and freedoms. Since the terrorist attacks

> *"Man's capacity for justice makes democracy possible, but man's inclination to injustice makes democracy necessary."*
>
> Reinhold Niebuhr, religious scholar and political philosopher (1892–1971). Quoted from the foreword of *Children of Light and Children of Darkness* (1944).

Israeli forces round up Palestinians suspected of terrorist attacks. The continuing conflicts between the Palestinians and the Israelis have placed enormous pressures on Israeli democracy. ▼

of September 11, 2001, many democratic states have introduced legislation to combat terrorism. Laws introduced, or being considered, involve the surveillance of suspects, imprisoning suspects without trial, lowering the standard of proof required to convict suspects, introducing national identity cards, seizing financial assets, and placing limits on freedom of speech.

These proposals have worried civil liberties groups because they undermine constitutional rights, such as the right to a fair trial and the right to privacy. Some also a fear that future governments might use these powers to suppress not just terrorists, but all political opposition. In this sense, terrorism poses a unique challenge to democracy. By confronting terrorism with the full power of the state, democratic governments may well have to consider abandoning—or at least modifying—some important democratic principles.

FUNDAMENTALISM

Since the late 1970s, there has been an upsurge in religious fundamentalism throughout the world. Fundamentalism is a movement that adopts a very strict interpretation of religious belief. There are fundamentalist movements within many of the world's major religions. Most fundamentalists despise the global trend towards secularism—that is, the decline of religion as a central guiding principle of government and law. Fundamentalists from certain religions—particularly Islam and Judaism—also reject the idea of democracy. These fundamentalists prefer instead that countries should be ruled by religious leaders, following laws laid down by God according to their sacred scriptures.

◄ On September 11, 2001, as part of a larger attack on the United States, two hijacked passenger planes were deliberately flown into the twin towers of the World Trade Center in New York City, causing them to collapse. The attacks killed about 3,000 people.

Jewish fundamentalists, also known as religious Zionists, would like Israel to be governed according to *halakah* (Jewish law). Similarly, Islamic fundamentalists, or Islamists, would like to see states governed according to their holy law, the *shariah*. These law systems allow no role for the will of the people and are therefore antidemocratic. Similarly, some Hindu fundamentalists favor a strict interpretation of their religion, which would give few rights to members of lower castes (hereditary classes into which Hindu society is divided).

Some fundamentalists are prepared to further their aims with violence and terrorism. Christian fundamentalists, however, usually fight their cause through legal and democratic means, although some antiabortion movements have resorted to violence. Some Christian fundamentalist goals (such as restricting the rights of homosexuals and forbidding the teaching of evolution) challenge democracy and the U.S. Constitution, which mandates religious freedom and a separation of church and state.

OSAMA BIN LADEN

Osama bin Laden is the leader of Al Qaeda, a global terrorist network. Al Qaeda has been behind some of the worst terrorist attacks of recent times, including those on September 11, 2001 in New York and Washington, D.C., and on passenger trains near Madrid, Spain in 2004. Bin Laden believes in an extreme, violent form of Islam. Like many other fundamentalists, he views Western society as deeply corrupt. In his opinion, liberal democratic attitudes have led people to indulge in sinful activities like drinking alcohol and taking drugs. Unlike the vast majority of Muslims, however, bin Laden is not willing to tolerate Western society, but wishes to destroy it. His ultimate aim is to re-establish the Caliphate—a united Islamic world under one central Islamic leadership. Then, he believes, Islam will be strong enough to defeat the West.

◀ Osama bin Laden, Islamic fundamentalist and fugitive leader of the terrorist network, Al Qaeda. In 1996 he declared war on the United States, and his organization is believed to have carried out the September 11, 2001, attack on New York City and Washington, D.C.

CHAPTER SIX

THE FUTURE OF DEMOCRACY

Democracy has grown enormously over the past hundred years. In 1900, there were no democracies in which all adults—women as well as men—could vote. In 2005, 120 out of 192 existing countries were electoral democracies, constituting 62.5 percent of the world's population. Not all of these democracies enjoy full rule of law and protection of human rights, but they do have democratic elections in place.

There is every reason to believe that this trend will continue. The importance of human rights—a basic principle of any democracy—is gaining global recognition. The widespread adoption of United Nations resolutions on such issues as torture, capital punishment, and the rights of religious minorities, women, children, and refugees, has helped promote a world culture in which democracy can flourish.

History also shows, however, that progress is never smooth or one-way. Ethnic and social divisions, an unstable economy, or an over-powerful military can often lead a newly democratic nation to slip back into authoritarianism. To be successful, new democracies require honest and principled political leaders; they need a professional class to fill key positions in the state, such as the judiciary and the civil service. They also require powerful, independent institutions, such as newspapers, other media, and trade unions, to act as a check on government and maintain a policy of free speech.

For those who believe that democracy is the best form of government, the goal for the next hundred years is generally to establish it as the dominant system of government throughout the world, as it already is in the West. For this to be achieved, the crucial problem of global poverty—and the vast inequality between wealthy and poor countries—needs to be addressed. It is particularly difficult for poorer countries to democ-ratize, because their people's priorities are food and shelter rather than political freedom. Also, widespread illiteracy makes it more difficult to build and maintain democratic institutions. Linking economic aid to political reform is therefore one way in which the West can help to further the spread of democracy to poorer countries. Another way is to assist poorer countries with training public officials such as election officers, constitutional lawyers, and members of the legislature. Emerging democracies can also be given advice on how to hold free and fair multi-party elections, and on how to ensure the practice of open and accountable government.

> *"Democracy is the worst form of government except all those other forms that have been tried from time to time."*
> British statesman Winston Churchill (1874–1965), from a speech given in Parliament on 11 November 1947.

▲ In 2004, students in Riga, Latvia, enjoy their democratic freedom to demonstrate against unpopular government policies. Until the country's independence from the USSR in 1991, such gatherings would have been illegal.

Western nations must continually monitor the health of their own democracies as they adapt to a changing world of globalization, increased immigration, and ethnic and religious diversity. If democracies curtail freedom of speech and right to trial in order to protect themselves, they lose the freedoms they are trying to protect. Democracy, although historically rare, has proved itself a long-lasting form of government, surviving all the global upheavals of the past hundred years. Now it must also meet the challenges of the twenty-first century and, perhaps, even be strengthened by them.

TIME LINE

C. 600S B.C.E.	ROMAN SENATE ESTABLISHED.
594 B.C.E.	SOLON, RULER OF ATHENS, INTRODUCES REFORMS, GIVING MORE POWER TO ORDINARY CITIZENS.
509 B.C.E.	ROMAN REPUBLIC FOUNDED.
508–502 B.C.E.	ATHENIAN STATESMAN, CLEISTHENES, ESTABLISHES DEMOCRACY IN ATHENS.
460–431 B.C.E.	PERICLES STRENGTHENS ATHENIAN DEMOCRACY.
C. 440 B.C.E.	ESTABLISHMENT OF ROMAN ASSEMBLY OF TRIBES.
431–404 B.C.E.	PELOPONNESIAN WAR BETWEEN ATHENS AND SPARTA WEAKENS ATHENIAN DEMOCRACY.
338 B.C.E.	GREEK CITIES CONQUERED BY MACEDON. MANY, INCLUDING ATHENS, CONTINUE TO FUNCTION AS DEMOCRACIES.
322 B.C.E.	FROM THIS TIME, MACEDONIAN KINGS START TO RULE GREEK CITIES DIRECTLY, CAUSING THE END OF GREEK DEMOCRACY.
27 B.C.E.	ROMAN REPUBLIC ENDS, TO BE REPLACED BY IMPERIAL GOVERNMENT.
600–1000 C.E.	VIKINGS NEAR TRONDHEIM REGULARLY MEET AT A *TING*, OR LOCAL ASSEMBLY.
C. 800	LOCAL POPULAR ASSEMBLY ESTABLISHED IN RAETIA (MODERN-DAY GRAUBÜNDEN, SWITZERLAND).
850–900	TINGS ESTABLISHED IN OTHER PARTS OF SCANDINAVIA.
930	ICELANDIC *ALTHING* ESTABLISHED.
1100S–C. 1350	RISE AND FALL OF CITY-REPUBLICS IN NORTHERN AND CENTRAL ITALY.
1215	KING JOHN SIGNS THE MAGNA CARTA.
1272–1307	ENGLISH PARLIAMENT ESTABLISHED.
1648	THE ENGLISH CIVIL WAR ENDS WITH A VICTORY FOR PARLIAMENT.
1649	CHARLES I, THE ENGLISH KING, IS EXECUTED.
1688	JAMES II IS DEPOSED AND EXILED.
1689	THE DECLARATION OF RIGHTS IS SIGNED.
1690	JOHN LOCKE PUBLISHES HIS INFLUENTIAL *TWO TREATISES*.
1762	JEAN-JACQUES ROUSSEAU WRITES *THE SOCIAL CONTRACT*.
1776	THE UNITED STATES DECLARES ITS INDEPENDENCE FROM GREAT BRITAIN. THE AMERICAN DECLARATION OF INDEPENDENCE IS DRAFTED.
1783	BRITAIN LOSES THE WAR OF INDEPENDENCE AND IS FORCED TO ACCEPT THE SOVEREIGNTY OF THE UNITED STATES.
1787	THE U.S. CONSTITUTION AND BILL OF RIGHTS ARE ESTABLISHED.
1789–99	THE FRENCH REVOLUTION DESTROYS THE FRENCH MONARCHY.
1832	BRITISH REFORM ACT EXTENDS THE FRANCHISE TO PROPERTIED, URBAN, MIDDLE-CLASS MEN. ELECTORATE INCREASES TO 650,000, 14 PERCENT OF ADULT MALES.

1833	SLAVERY IS ABOLISHED THROUGHOUT THE BRITISH EMPIRE.
1848	A YEAR OF REVOLUTIONS PREVAILS THROUGHOUT EUROPE.
1859	JOHN STEWART MILL PUBLISHES *ON LIBERTY*.
1866	SLAVERY ABOLISHED IN THE UNITED STATES.
1867	BRITISH REFORM ACT EXTENDS THE FRANCHISE TO 1,500,000 MEN, 40 PERCENT OF ADULT MALES.
1869	WYOMING BECOMES THE FIRST TERRITORY IN MODERN TIMES TO GIVE WOMEN THE VOTE.
1871	GERMANY INTRODUCES UNIVERSAL MALE SUFFRAGE.
1884	BRITISH REFORM ACT EXTENDS FRANCHISE TO 5.5 MILLION MEN, 60 PERCENT OF ADULT MALES.
1893	NEW ZEALAND OFFERS WOMEN THE VOTE, BECOMING THE FIRST NATION IN HISTORY TO ESTABLISH UNIVERSAL SUFFRAGE.
1917	COMMUNIST REGIME TAKES POWER IN RUSSIA.
1918	BRITISH REFORM ACT EXTENDS FRANCHISE TO ALL ADULT MALES AND TO WOMEN OVER THE AGE OF 30.
1920	U.S. WOMEN WIN THE RIGHT TO VOTE.
1922	FASCIST REGIME TAKES POWER IN ITALY.
1924	TURKEY BECOMES A DEMOCRACY.
1928	ALL BRITISH WOMEN OVER THE AGE OF 21 WIN RIGHT TO VOTE.
1933	THE FASCIST NAZI REGIME TAKES POWER IN GERMANY.
1945	FASCIST STATES OF GERMANY AND JAPAN DEFEATED IN WORLD WAR II.
1946	DEMOCRACY ESTABLISHED IN JAPAN.
1948	INDIA BECOMES THE WORLD'S LARGEST DEMOCRACY. ISRAEL BECOMES THE FIRST STABLE DEMOCRACY IN THE MIDDLE EAST. THE UN APPROVES THE UNIVERSAL DECLARATION OF HUMAN RIGHTS.
1960s	CIVIL RIGHTS MOVEMENT IN THE UNITED STATES BRINGS POLITICAL EQUALITY TO AFRICAN AMERICANS.
1989	PRODEMOCRACY DEMONSTRATIONS TIANANMEN SQUARE, BEIJING, CHINA, MAKE GLOBAL NEWS.
1989—1991	COLLAPSE OF EUROPEAN COMMUNISM IS FOLLOWED BY THE SUBSEQUENT RISE OF DEMOCRACY IN RUSSIA AND EASTERN EUROPE.
1994	MULTIRACIAL DEMOCRATIC ELECTIONS ARE HELD IN SOUTH AFRICA, ENDING THE BRUTAL SYSTEM OF RACIAL SEGREGATION KNOWN AS APARTHEID.
1999	NIGERIA AND INDONESIA ELECT DEMOCRATIC GOVERNMENTS.
2004	DEMOCRATIC ELECTIONS TAKE PLACE IN AFGHANISTAN.
2005	DEMOCRATIC ELECTIONS TAKE PLACE IN IRAQ.

Glossary

authoritarian/authoritarianism a nondemocratic style of government that requires obedience to a ruling person or group

cabinet a group of senior members of a government, appointed by a chief executive to take responsibility for specific areas of policy

chiefdom territory controlled by a tribe and led by a chief

city-state an independent state consisting of a city and its surrounding territory

civil service all the governmental departments of a state and the employees who work in them.

coalition the temporary union of two or more groups for a particular purpose, such as a campaign

Cold War the state of nonviolent conflict between the Soviet Union and the United States and their respective allies between 1945 and 1990

colony a territory ruled by another country

communism a system, or the belief in a system, in which capitalism is overthrown and the state controls wealth and property

Congress the national legislative body of the United States, consisting of the House of Representatives and the Senate

conservative describing a political or religious outlook that desires to keep things as they are and to preserve traditional ways of life

constituency a group of citizens living in an electoral district who are entitled to elect someone of that district to represent them in government

constitutional monarchy a political system in which the monarch's powers, rights, and duties are limited and defined by law

decolonization granting independence to a colony or colonies

developed countries the more technologically advanced, wealthy countries of the world

developing countries the poorer countries of the world that lack the capital and technology to make use of available resources

dictatorship government by a leader who rules the country with absolute power, usually by force

divine right the belief that a monarch's authority comes directly from God rather than from the people

Enlightenment an eighteenth-century movement in Western Europe that emphasized the use of reason and science in human life and culture

ethnic minority a group with a similar cultural background that forms a minority in a country

executive the branch of government responsible for making and implementing policy

fascism a political movement that favors centralized, dictatorial government and the repression of political opposition; Fascists tend to hold nationalistic, often racist, views and to believe in strong leadership that does not tolerate dissent

federal a form of government in which several states give up certain powers to a central authority, but also have limited powers to run their own affairs

heredity a system in which the leadership of a country, religion, or other institution is passed on from one generation to the next

impeach to charge a person with wrongdoing in office before an official tribunal: Impeachment can result in removal from office

Industrial Revolution the period beginning in the second half of the eighteenth century when Britain, Europe, and the United States enjoyed a surge in productivity and wealth due to the widespread adoption of large-scale, mechanical means of production

International Court of Justice the chief court of the United Nations, which rules on disputes between member nations who bring a case to court

International Monetary Fund an agency of the United Nations that seeks to promote international cooperation between countries on financial matters

juror a person who serves on a jury

jury a group of people, usually numbering twelve, chosen to give a verdict on a legal case that is presented to them in a court of law

liberal describing a belief in freedom of thought, speech, action, and religion, and tolerance towards others

lobbying attempting to persuade a politician to support a particular cause

militant extremely active in support of a cause, often to an extent that causes conflict or even violence with other people or institutions

nation-state an independent, sovereign state recognized by other states and able to interact with them

nobility a high-ranking class of people in a country, who achieved their status through birth within the noble class

parliament the name of the legislative body in many democratic countries

radical supportive of extreme political, economic, or social change

republic another word for democracy; that is, a system of government in which people elect representatives to exercise power for them

revolution violent overthrow of a ruler or political system

sovereignty supreme authority over a state

Soviet Union also known as the Union of Soviet Socialist Republics (USSR), a country formed from the territories of the Russian Empire in 1917, which lasted until 1991

trade unions organizations established to help workers get and maintain fair wages, benefits, working conditions, and protection in their own trade or industry

tyrant a ruler with absolute power, who exercises authority cruelly and unjustly

United Nations an organization representing the world's nations and often involved in intervening in international crises with aid and peacekeeping forces

Western countries countries of North America and Europe that became powerful during the eighteenth and nineteenth centuries and that are now characterized by secular and generally liberal culture, advanced technology and infrastructure, and a democratic form of government

World Bank an agency of the United Nations that guarantees loans to member nations for the purpose of reconstruction and development

BOOKS

Beetham, David. and Kevin Boyle. *Introducing Democracy: 80 Questions and Answers.* UNESCO, 2002.

Coleman, Stephen. *Citizen Guides: What Happens in Parliament.* Franklin Watts, 2003.

Downing, David. *Political and Economic Systems: Democracy.* Heinemann, 2003.

Harris, Nathaniel. *Democracy.* Ideas of the Modern World (series). Raintree, 2001.

Ling, Bettina. *Aung San Suu Kyi: Standing Up for Democracy in Burma.* Feminist Press, 1999.

WEB SITES

www.pbs.org/democracy/kids/

www.fairvote.org/

congressforkids.net/Independence_democracy.htm

www.kidsnewsroom.org/newsissues/071103/index.asp?page = AroundWorld

www.kidsdomain.com/holiday/july4/decl.html

http://congressforkids.net/Independence_declaration_1.htm

INDEX

DEMCO